KALE

The Secret Key to Vibrant Health

First published in Great Britain in 2016 by Modern Books
An imprint of Elwin Street Limited
3 Percy Street
London W1T 1DE
www.elwinstreet.com

ISBN 978-1-906761-81-3
6 7 8 9 10   5 4 3 2 1

Originally published under the title: *Kale, un super aliment dans votre assiette*
By Claire 'Clea' Chapoutot © 2014 by Éditions La Plage, Paris

Translator: Drew Smith

ABOUT THE AUTHOR
Claire 'Clea' Chapoutot is a French food blogger (cleacuisine.fr) who specializes in healthy eating and vegetarian cuisine. She is a prize-winning author of numerous books, including *Matcha*, which is forthcoming in the Natural Superfoods series.

Picture Credits:
Photographs by Emma Dufraisseix, except Alamy: © Andrea Jones Images, 9, © Food Centrale Hamburg GmbH, 14, © Helen Sessions, 5; Getty Images: © Frederic J. Brown/Staff, 10, © James Ross, 6; Shutterstock: © Brent Hofacker, 42.

Printed in China

NATURAL 🌿 SUPERFOODS

KALE

The Secret Key to Vibrant Health

Claire Chapoutot

CONTENTS

SECTION 1: DISCOVER KALE

SECTION 2: RAW KALE RECIPES

SECTION 3: COOKED KALE RECIPES

DISCOVER KALE

Packed with fibre, but low in calories, kale rates as one of today's superfoods. You'll see it on restaurant menus, in blogs and as the star of the latest cookbooks. In just a few years kale has replaced romaine lettuce and spinach as the king of greens. This book will teach you about the different varieties and the nutritional value of this versatile leaf, and show you how to use kale in a wide variety of raw and cooked dishes.

SUPREME GREENS

Not so long ago, finding kale in a farmer's market was not that easy. It was just another of those forgotten, overlooked vegetables like purple sprouting broccoli or crosnes. Not anymore, however. Today, kale sits proudly on the salad shelves in the supermarket. Better still, kale is cheap. It is a wild cabbage that is easily grown and has been for millennia.

HEALTHY KALE

So what makes kale so special? For starters, kale is incredibly good for you. Secondly, it takes very little effort to prepare. Simply cut the leaves in two or three slices, rinse them gently and then – perhaps somewhat surprisingly – massage the leaves. To eat kale raw, it must be kneaded by hand to break down its fibres and tenderize it. Once that's done, all that remains is to mix the leaves with a lemon-infused vinaigrette for a delicious salad.

As mentioned, kale is not only easy to prepare, but also packed with nutritional goodness. Like all cruciferous cabbages, kale is very low in calories and high in fibre, which makes it perfect for detoxing. Yet what earns kale its title of 'super-cabbage' are its incredible levels of trace elements, vitamins and antioxidants. Kale is, without a doubt, the king of greens!

Kale has more vitamin C than an orange; two handfuls of kale leaves hold more than 100% of your recommended daily intake of vitamin C. This magic green is also rich in vitamin A and vitamin K, and contains more calcium than a glass of milk (150 mg per 100 g kale against 125 mg in a glass of milk). Kale has twice the number of antioxidants found in other green leafy vegetables, in particular lutein and zeaxanthin, which help prevent cataracts, macular degeneration and glaucoma.

Furthermore, kale contains sulforaphane, a potent anticarcinogenic which helps to fight against inflammation of the stomach and blood vessels. Scientists also see it having a role to play in the fight against diseases such as cancer, Alzheimer's and even depression.

TASTY KALE

I confess that I used to be a little bit anti-cabbage in the kitchen. Sure those little leaves might be bursting with benefits, but so what? I found it took me two weeks to get through a whole white cabbage, and for a while they were banned from my vegetable box. Instead my choice was always for easier ingredients, such as chard, spinach or lettuce. And when the craze for kale first began, championed by Hollywood stars such as Gwyneth Paltrow, Heidi Klum and Jennifer Aniston, I still refused to take an interest.

And then one day I was given a huge box of kale by a gardener friend of mine and, out of politeness, I was forced to find a use for it. It turned out to be so easy to work with, so simple to wash, slice and cook. I was also surprised that it had no sulphur smell to it

Most kale varieties have green leaves, sometimes tinged with purple.

either. It took me a few days, but I finally had to admit I was in love! And I was addicted!

I tried out every recipe I could find and discovered a wealth of delicious ideas. Raw kale is not unlike spinach, even if it needs a little more chewing. Cooked, it becomes tender and a little tart, more like chard in flavour, or lemony, bitter sorrel. And it is so incredibly versatile. The leaves can be eaten raw or steamed in savoury dishes; they juice brilliantly well and can even be tucked into some surprising desserts, such as ice cream and chocolate fondant.

KALE VARIETIES

The variety of kale found most frequently on the supermarket shelves, is 'curly kale'. True to its common name, this does have very curly, crenellated leaves. But look out for other varieties, such as the longer 'dinosaur' or Tuscan black kale (cavolo nero) whose broad leaves are ideal for rolling up around a stuffing. There are also Red Russian and Redbor varieties which are virtually purple.

IN THE KITCHEN

Eating kale raw makes the most of its vitamins and antioxidants. It can be mixed into smoothies, juices, spreads and pesto with barely any work at all. You can also just steam or stew it for a couple of minutes. This will soften the leaves without losing too many nutrients – handy if you want to add a little colour and vitamins to a rice or pasta dish.

EATING KALE RAW

For salads, and any other dishes that feature raw kale, the leaves should be 'massaged' to soften them and break down their fibres. This makes the leaves much more pleasant to chew. To do this, simply mix the leaves in a bowl with a vinaigrette, a runny cream sauce or a simple mixture of olive oil and lemon juice. Mix with both hands, rubbing the leaves with your fingers as if making a crumble topping or pastry. Don't be too gentle. Kale likes a really vigorous massage!

After massaging well, the leaves will reduce in volume and your salad will be ready to eat.

COOKING WITH KALE

Kale tastes equally delicious when stewed, steamed, stir-fried, deep-fried or added to soups. And you'll find crispy, oven-baked kale chips are utterly addictive! After trying out some of the wonderful dishes in this book you'll be sure to discover that kale is your new best friend. Here you'll not only find filling and tasty casseroles, lasagnes

Kale is considered a superfood, alongside spinach, cucumber, celery and lemon.

and pies, but also sweeter treats such as breads, cakes and desserts. I am sure you'll find a recipe here to suit every taste and every occasion.

Kale marries perfectly with garlic, ginger and lemon. It also works well with cereals and pulses in stews and soups. Its raw texture befriends fruits such as avocado, citrus, apple, pomegranate or red fruits. Nuts, such as hazelnuts, almonds, cashews and walnuts add depth to its flavour, whether raw or cooked themselves. And, both in terms of colour and taste, kale fraternizes easily with onions, squash, root vegetables (such as carrots and beetroot) and mushrooms. And like all green vegetables, kale goes very well with cheese and eggs.

Kale stems need to be cut into very small pieces when cooked. They can be used in casseroles, soups or any other recipes that require long cooking, but I prefer to use them just for vegetable stock and soups.

Shiny and wiry leaves are the watchword when shopping for kale.

STORING KALE

Kale will keep for about a week in the salad drawer of the refrigerator. But keep it dark and even wrap it in a cloth. To wash it, I recommend separating the leaves from the stalks, which is easy. Just slice down the stem and let the leaf fall away. Then just rinse the leaves under running water, as you might for lettuce, and dry them in a spinner.

For longer-term storage kale leaves can be frozen and thawed very easily. Either put the leaves straight into freezer bags and store them as they are, or liquidize, cooked or raw, to a purée with just a little water and portion them up in an ice-cube tray. Prepared like this kale will keep for up to three months in the freezer.

And a kale ice cube dropped into a soup – hot or cold – will add a wonderful burst of flavour and colour.

USING THIS BOOK

A single kale stem with leaves weighs about 50–60 g. When the stem is removed you will be left with about 30 g of leaf – a generous handful. For all the recipes in this book, the term 'kale leaves' means the leaves without the stem and weights are given assuming the stems have already been removed.

GROWING YOUR OWN

SEEDS

Kale seed can be bought very easily over the internet or at most garden centres. There are several varieties available such as Red Russian (a hardy plant with tender leaves) Dwarf Green Curled (good for dry, windswept gardens), Redbor (frilly leaves that make excellent salads) or the well-known dark green leaves of Nero di Toscana.

SOWING, TRANSPLANTING AND PLANTING

Sow the seeds from April to June in a suitable compost and make sure they are well sheltered. When the seedling has four leaves on it, transplant into pots. Kale is less demanding than many other species of brassica and it adapts to any type of soil, but it needs some feed in the soil and really appreciates a good sunny spot.

The plants are ready for the garden when they have at least 6–8 leaves each (usually around three to four weeks after potting). Plant at a distance of 50 cm apart and sink deeply into the ground, leaving 2 cm at the base of the leaves. Water thoroughly and mulch the soil.

CARING FOR GROWING PLANTS

Keep an eye on the soil and ensure that it does not get too dry. Kale likes to stay fresh and watered. Kale has the advantage having hardly any pests but you may get bugs (such as *Nezara viridula*) that have to be taken off by hand.

WHEN TO HARVEST

It usually takes around 4–6 months from sowing to harvest. When ready you can take the leaves one by one according to your needs, always selecting leaves from the bottom of the stem. Harvest after the first frost, so the leaves are fuller in flavour.

Keep seedlings indoors or in a greenhouse until they are ready for the garden – usually around 3–4 weeks.

RAW KALE RECIPES

Add a new twist to salads and sandwiches with a handful of shredded kale leaves. They work particularly well with creamy dressings and the sharp flavours of feta and goat's cheese. Juice the leaves for a glass of raw energy or blend them for making kale hummus and pesto. As with many vegetables, kale is at its nutritional best in its raw state. Eaten in moderation, it will contribute substantially to a weekly diet in terms of fibre, antioxidants and vitamins A, C and K.

AUTUMN SALAD WITH BEETROOT AND PINE NUTS

The combination of kale with root vegetables is fantastic, especially when the root vegetables are roasted. Here they are topped with a miso-tahini sauce and served warm.

SERVES 4

2 raw beetroot, peeled and cubed

Olive oil and lemon juice for drizzling

4 tablespoons pine nuts

3 tablespoons tahini

1 tablespoon miso

6 handfuls of kale leaves

1 apple, peeled, cored and diced

3 tablespoons dried cranberries

Salt

Preheat the oven to 180°C/Gas mark 4.

Drizzle the beetroot with olive oil and lemon juice and sprinkle with salt. Bake for at least 30 minutes. About 8 minutes before the end of cooking, add the pine nuts.

In a large bowl, combine the tahini and the miso. Thin with a little hot water to make a smooth, creamy sauce. Add the kale leaves and 'massage' them vigorously with both hands to coat them with the sauce.

Once the beetroot is cooked, transfer to a large serving dish. Add the kale, diced apple and cranberries. Serve warm or cold.

GOOD TO KNOW: As winter comes on you can include other vegetables in this dish. Try carrots, squash or cauliflower.

WINTER SALAD WITH ORANGE AND FETA

SERVES 4

120 g walnuts

1 garlic clove, crushed

2 teaspoons mustard

2 teaspoons cider vinegar

2 tablespoons olive oil

1 teaspoon honey

6 kale leaves, roughly chopped

2 oranges, peeled and cut into segments, reserving any juice

1 grapefruit, peeled and cut into segments, reserving any juice

200 g feta cheese, crumbled

Salt and pepper

Kale is particularly tasty in combination with feta cheese and citrus fruit. With some roasted nuts to add crunch, this salad has a delicious, warming touch.

Preheat the oven to 180°C/Gas mark 4 and roast the nuts for 8 minutes.

In a large bowl, combine the garlic with the mustard. Mix with the reserved citrus juice, vinegar, oil and honey. Season to taste.

Add the kale leaves to the bowl. Toss with the sauce and 'massage' with both hands until the leaves are tender.

Halve the orange and grapefruit segments and add to the bowl, along with the feta and roasted nuts.

VARIATION: Kale pairs divinely with all citrus fruits – try mandarin wedges or even slices of lemon sprinkled with spices and caramelized in the oven.

SUMMER SALAD WITH FIGS AND POMEGRANATE

Try this wonderful summery mix of kale leaves with pomegranate seeds and figs. The cheese adds extra texture and zingy freshness to the salad.

SERVES 4

1 teaspoon honey

1 teaspoon strong mustard

Pinch of salt

2 teaspoons balsamic vinegar

2 teaspoons nut oil

1 teaspoon olive oil

6 large fresh, new-season kale leaves

1 pomegranate, seeded

Handful of nuts

6 fresh figs, each cut into 8

150 g goat's cheese, diced

In a large salad bowl, combine the honey, mustard and salt. Blend in the vinegar and the oils.

Give the kale leaves a good rub between your hands and then add them to the bowl and work the vinaigrette into the leaves. Add the pomegranate seeds to the bowl.

Lightly fry the nuts in a dry frying pan over a medium heat and shake off any skins. Roughly chop or crush the warm nuts.

Add the nuts, fig pieces and diced cheese to the bowl. Mix everything to combine and serve immediately.

VARIATION: When the first leaves of kale are harvested at the end of summer they are vital and less sweet than later in the year. Make the most of them by substituting tomatoes and raspberries for the figs and pomegranate.

CAESAR SALAD WITH KALE

SERVES 4

For the salad

8 kale leaves, chopped

1 romaine lettuce, shredded

80 g Parmesan cheese shavings

12 Kalamata olives

⅓ baguette, cut into small cubes

Olive oil

Salt and pepper

For the sauce

100 g walnuts, pecans or cashew nuts, soaked in water

2 garlic cloves, chopped

4 Kalamata olives, pitted

1 tablespoon mustard

100 ml lemon juice

4 tablespoons olive oil or a little milk

Salt and pepper

A real Caesar salad combines egg with anchovy sauce, bacon and chicken, but it is the combination of crunchy leaves with creamy sauce, the sweetness of the Parmesan and the crisp croutons that we really tend to remember. Kale is perfect for this vegetarian version of the old classic.

For the sauce, first drain the nuts and mix with the remaining sauce ingredients, then refrigerate.

In a large bowl, massage the kale leaves with the creamy sauce. Add the romaine lettuce, Parmesan shavings and olives.

Preheat the grill. Place the bread cubes in a baking dish. Season with salt and pepper and brush with olive oil.

Toast under the grill for 5–10 minutes.

Toss the croutons with the salad and serve immediately.

GOOD TO KNOW: The night before making this salad, soak the nuts for 10 minutes (walnuts or pecans) or four hours (cashews) in a large container filled with water.

KALE TABBOULEH

Tabbouleh is an all-time classic. There is a difference between French tabbouleh – rich in cereals – and that from North Africa, which is richer in herbs. This kale version sits in the middle. My personal twist is adding the roasted almonds.

SERVES 4

150 g bulgur wheat

2 tablespoons olive oil

4 tablespoons lemon juice

200 g kale leaves, sliced

Handful of parsley, chopped

Handful of mint, chopped

12 vine tomatoes, halved

1 small cucumber, peeled and diced

3 spring onions, finely chopped

½ preserved lemon, finely chopped

50 g raisins

60 g almonds

Salt

Cook the bulgur wheat in double the volume of water for 5 minutes. Sprinkle with salt and leave to swell, covered, for 15 minutes.

In a large salad bowl, mix the olive oil, lemon juice and a pinch of salt. Add the kale and massage the oil mix into the leaves. Add to the bulgur wheat.

Add the remaining ingredients to the bowl, except for the almonds. Chill in the refrigerator for at least four hours and up to two days.

Preheat the oven to 180°C/Gas mark 4. Roast the almonds for 10 minutes. Once cool, crush the nuts into small pieces and add to the rest of the salad just before serving.

VARIATIONS: You can use any grain you like for this recipe – bulgur wheat, quinoa or couscous (which doesn't need separate cooking). In winter, try replacing the tomatoes and cucumber with grapefruit or orange.

DEHYDRATED KALE CHIPS

Kale chips have helped popularize this wonderful vegetable. Light and crisp, they are super-easy to make at home either in the bottom of the oven at a low temperature or using a dehydrator.

SERVES 4

Handful of kale leaves

4 tablespoons lemon juice

2–3 tablespoons olive oil

Salt

For a sweet marinade

2 tablespoons tahini

3 tablespoons fresh orange juice

1 tablespoon agave syrup

1 teaspoon soy sauce

Separate the kale leaves, wash and massage well. In a large salad bowl, mix the leaves with the lemon juice, olive oil and a little salt.

Lay the leaves on the shelves of a dehydrator. Dry at 40°C for 12 hours. The chips should be crisp and crackling.

To make sweet kale chips, follow the method above, replacing the savoury mix for a sweet marinade.

GOOD TO KNOW: You can play around with other spices – salty and sweet. Try cinnamon, ginger, cocoa, pimento.

KALE JUICE

When it comes to juicing, kale is unrivalled. Not only does it give a drink the most vibrant green hue, but it packs a powerful nutritional punch, too.

MOCKTAIL MOJITO

Blend a handful of kale leaves with half a bunch of mint (retaining a few leaves for garnishing) and a little water. Strain the mixture and dilute with sparkling water, the juice of 4 limes and 3 tablespoons of agave syrup or honey. Serve with ice cubes, lime slices and mint leaves. This recipe makes enough to serve eight people.

GREEN ZINGER

Feed 2 kale leaves into a juicer, one at a time, followed by half a peeled and chopped pineapple, 2 chopped red apples and a 2-cm piece of peeled fresh root ginger. Add the juice of 1 lime and a little water if necessary. Serve cold. This recipe makes enough to serve four people.

KALE HUMMUS

SERVES 4

240 g canned chickpeas

80 g kale leaves, chopped

1 tablespoon miso

2 tablespoons tahini

2 garlic cloves, crushed

2 tablespoons olive oil

4 tablespoons lemon juice

Try this hummus on bread for an open sandwich, on toast or in a wrap.

Rinse the chickpeas under running water until the water runs clear. Remove any skins and place in a blender with the kale. Add the remaining ingredients and blend to your desired consistency. You can make a purée or leave a few larger pieces for a chunky finish. For an even smoother finish you can add a little water or natural yogurt.

KALE PESTO

Stir this pesto into pasta or spread it over the base of a veggie pizza.

SERVES 4

50 g nuts

50 g Parmesan cheese, grated

50 g kale leaves, chopped

80 ml olive oil

Fry the nuts for 8 minutes in a dry pan over a medium heat. Remove the skins and place the nuts in a blender. Add the Parmesan, kale and olive oil. Blend for long enough to achieve a smooth purée.

GOOD TO KNOW: This pesto will keep in the refrigerator for one week. Alternatively, freeze it in an ice-cube tray for up to one month.

CHOCOLATE MINT ICE CREAM

Don't say a word when you serve this! No one needs to know that it contains kale (and no one will notice, even if you use a lot). It will add a lovely sweet tang, its deep green colour and all of its nutrition.

SERVES 6

50 g kale leaves, finely chopped

15 g mint leaves

120 ml almond milk

4 tablespoons agave syrup

1 heaped tablespoon white almond purée

500 g Greek yogurt

75 g plain chocolate, broken into shards

Place the kale in the bowl of a blender with the mint leaves, almond milk and agave syrup. Blend.

Add the white almond purée and the yogurt and blend again. Place the bowl in the refrigerator for at least six hours, then transfer the ice cream to an ice-cream maker for 20–30 minutes, adding the chocolate shards towards the end.

Transfer the mix to a bowl and place in the freezer for at least 5 minutes before serving. If you are keeping the ice cream in the freezer for a few days, take it out 10–15 minutes ahead of time.

GOOD TO KNOW: You can make a vegan version of this ice cream. Simply swap the yogurt for smooth tofu.

KALE FAJITA WRAPS WITH AVOCADO AND CRANBERRY

Wraps are great and can be filled with anything and everything that you have to hand. This creamy avocado sauce goes divinely with the kale.

SERVES 3

100 g kale leaves

½ avocado, diced

25 g mixed nuts or cashew nuts

25 g cranberries

6 wraps

For the sauce

½ avocado

1 tablespoon lime juice

1 teaspoon soy sauce

2 tablespoons nut oil

Small tub natural soya yogurt

Place all the sauce ingredients in a blender and blend to a cream. Transfer the mix to a salad bowl, add the kale and massage the sauce into the leaves using your hands. Add the avocado to the salad bowl along with the nuts and cranberries.

Lay a wrap out on a flat surface and fill with the salad. Roll up. Assemble all of the wraps in this way. Keep the wraps in the refrigerator for a few hours – they will not lose shape – or serve immediately.

GOOD TO KNOW: You can use up any leftovers in a salad with chickpeas, tomato slices, cooked beetroot and grated carrot.

KALE AND APPLE SANDWICHES WITH GOAT'S CHEESE

Enjoy this marriage of apple and kale, mustard and cheese.

SERVES 1

1 teaspoon Meaux or Dijon mustard

1 teaspoon cider vinegar

1 tablespoon olive oil

Handful of kale leaves, finely chopped

2 slices of bread

6 walnuts, roughly chopped

40 g goat's cheese, finely sliced

½ red apple, thinly sliced and any pips removed

Salt and pepper

In a small bowl, mix the mustard with a little salt, the vinegar and olive oil. Give it a grind of pepper.

Add the kale to the bowl and massage the vinaigrette into the leaves for a couple of minutes using your fingers.

Lay out one slice of bread with a layer of kale, then cheese, then nuts and then apple.

Top the sandwich with the second slice of bread, press down gently and eat straight away.

VARIATIONS: You can add other elements as you like – for example, chopped, dried apricots or prunes. Grated carrot works just as well as apple.

CUCUMBER AND KALE CEVICHE

This soup takes advantage of all the nutritional virtues of kale. Serve it in shot glasses as an aperitif, in little bowls as a starter or as a dip with coconut cream and crackers.

SERVES 4

150 ml coconut milk

1 tablespoon miso

250 ml warm water

1 avocado, peeled and pitted

100 g kale leaves, chopped

1 tablespoon chopped coriander

1 cucumber, peeled, seeded and roughly chopped

Salt

Place the coconut milk in a blender. Mix the miso with a little of the warm water to dissolve, then add the rest of the water and pour into the blender.

Add the avocado, kale and coriander. Blend, check the seasoning and add a little salt or more water as desired.

Add the cucumber to the blender and pulse again until smooth. Serve chilled.

GOOD TO KNOW: Avocado, coconut and coriander always go well together, but experiment with other variations, too, like almond milk with basil or mint.

KALE SMOOTHIES

Kale is king of the quick green smoothie, milder and sweeter than either spinach or parsley. Those who are not converted to the benefits of pure greenness can always spike their drinks with chocolate or blueberries. Each recipe serves one.

BANANA SMOOTHIE
In a blender, combine 1 banana, 30 g kale leaves and 200 ml almond or soya milk. Drink straight away.

AVOCADO SMOOTHIE
In a blender, combine ½ avocado, 1 kiwifruit, peeled, 30 g kale leaves, 1 bunch of parsley, leaves only, 1 teaspoon agave syrup and 200 ml almond or rice milk. Drink straight away.

RED FRUIT SMOOTHIE
In a blender, combine ½ avocado, ½ banana, 30 g kale leaves, 60 g raspberries, 1 tablespoon tahini, 1 teaspoon chia seeds and 200 ml almond or rice milk. Drink straight away.

COCONUT SMOOTHIE
In a blender, combine 30 g kale leaves, 60 g blueberries or cherries (stoned), 2 teaspoons coconut flakes, 1 teaspoon honey or agave syrup and 1 small tub soya yogurt with vanilla. Drink straight away.

COOKED
KALE RECIPES

This inspired selection of recipes exploits the benefits of eating kale when cooked – even if only lightly so. Sometimes, a few minutes in the oven for a crispy finish or simple wilting before being blended into a soup is all it takes. When cooked for longer, kale also marries well with hearty fare, such as root vegetables, mushrooms and lentils, and adds an extra dimension to classic dishes like lasagne and pizza. Although cooking kale reduces its nutritional value, it does not diminish the cholesterol-lowering impact of this leafy green.

KALE AND BEETROOT BRUSCHETTA

Serve these hot toasts with a good bowl of soup or a large salad. Alternatively, slice them into bite-sized pieces and pass around with an aperitif.

SERVES 4

120 g cooked beetroot, peeled and diced

2 dates, diced

40 g walnuts

2 tablespoons nut oil

1 shallot, peeled and diced

4 slices of good-quality sourdough bread

60 g kale leaves, finely chopped

4 tablespoons lemon juice

10 g goat's cheese, sliced into rounds

Preheat the oven to 180°C/Gas mark 4.

In a medium bowl, mix the beetroot with the dates, walnuts and nut oil. Add the diced shallot to the mix.

Spread the mix on to the bread and bake for 5 minutes. While it is cooking, massage the kale with the lemon juice.

Take the bread slices out of the oven, cover with kale and top with rounds of goat's cheese. Return to the oven for 5 minutes. Serve hot.

GOOD TO KNOW: A bruschetta traditionally involves a slice of sourdough bread, rubbed with garlic, grilled and topped with tomato, basil and mozzarella.

STUFFED KALE

This marriage of tempeh, coconut milk, lime and peanuts, is like taking a holiday in the South Seas. Tempeh is a fermented bean product developed in Indonesia, Southeast Asia.

SERVES 4

250 g tempeh

1 tablespoon peanut butter

2 tablespoons lime juice

1 tablespoon soy sauce

1.5-cm piece fresh root ginger, peeled and diced

1 garlic clove, diced

2 tablespoons coconut milk

16 Tuscan kale (cavolo nero) leaves

160 g brown basmati rice

Crushed peanuts, to serve

The night before serving this recipe, cut the tempeh into 16 batons. In a shallow dish, mix the peanut butter with the lime juice and the soy sauce. Add the ginger and the garlic. Stir in the coconut milk.

Add the tempeh batons to the marinade, turning them over a few times to coat, cover and leave the dish in the refrigerator overnight.

By morning the tempeh should have absorbed the marinade ingredients. Roll each baton inside a kale leaf. Steam the kale parcels for 10 minutes, or until warmed through.

Cook the rice according to the instructions on the packet. Spoon some rice on to a plate, top with a stuffed kale parcel and garnish with peanuts.

GOOD TO KNOW: Tuscan black kale leaves are big enough to take a plump stuffing and still hold together for steaming. If you have big enough curly kale leaves, these can work too.

QUICK KALE SOUP WITH OATS

This soup is really quick to make and only needs enough time for the kale to wilt and the oats to swell. Serve it as it comes or upgrade with cubes of avocado, tomato, grilled chickpeas, garlic croutons or sliced cheese.

SERVES 2

1 tablespoon olive oil

1 small onion, peeled and chopped

4 kale leaves

4 tablespoons oats

200 ml almond milk

2 tablespoons soft cheese (optional)

Salt and pepper

Heat the oil in a saucepan and add the onion. Lightly fry until golden, then add the kale and the oats. Pour in 100 ml water and cover.

Cook over a low heat for 5 minutes or until the kale wilts. Add the almond milk (and a tablespoon of cheese per person if you want to make the soup more creamy).

Season with salt and pepper. Serve warm.

CROQUE-MADAME WITH KALE AND SUN-DRIED TOMATOES

The kale here is cooked with finely chopped sun-dried tomatoes and lifted with a little mustard. Cook the egg as you like it. It brings a sense of the unctuousness and mellow to everything. Serve with a green salad.

SERVES 4

4 tablespoons olive oil, plus extra for frying

80 g kale leaves, roughly chopped

8 sun-dried tomatoes, roughly chopped

8 slices of sourdough bread

4 tablespoons grain mustard

4 eggs

Salt and pepper

Warm the olive oil in a saucepan. Add the kale and tomatoes and leave to sweat over a low heat for 3–4 minutes.

Grill four slices of bread. Spread each slice with mustard, then top with the kale. Grill the other four slices and set aside.

Fry the eggs in oil. Season them, and lay them on top of the kale. Finish each sandwich with a second slice of bread.

Press down lightly without breaking the egg. In a dry pan over a medium heat, sear the sandwiches for 2 minutes on each side. Serve hot.

KALE AND CASHEW PASTA SAUCE

This is my version of sauce Alfredo. Originally Alfredo was a sauce of cream and cheese, spiked with garlic. Vegans all around the world have developed no-cheese versions, and this is my favourite.

SERVES 2

50 g cashew nuts

200 g spaghetti, spelt if possible

2 tablespoons malted yeast

1 teaspoon mustard

2 teaspoons lemon juice

1 garlic clove, diced

50 g kale leaves, finely chopped

Salt and pepper

Soak the cashew nuts in water for at least 6 hours. Drain. Cook the pasta according to the packet instructions.

Meanwhile, in a medium bowl, mix the cashew nuts with the yeast, mustard and lemon juice. Add the garlic to the mix. Add two-thirds of the kale to the bowl and season.

When the pasta is cooked, drain and return to the pan. Mix in the sauce and the remaining raw kale. Cook for another 3 minutes and serve very hot.

GOOD TO KNOW: Once cashew nuts have soaked for a few hours, they blend easily with the other ingredients and give the sauce a cheese-like flavour and texture.

QUINOA WITH MISO-KALE SAUCE

SERVES 4

240 g quinoa

1 onion, peeled and chopped

250 g mushrooms, chopped

1 tablespoon olive oil

2 bay leaves

75 ml stock (vegetable, herb or miso)

Handful of kale leaves, chopped

For the miso sauce

Small handful of kale leaves, sliced

2 teaspoons miso

120 g silken tofu, drained and crumbled

2 tablespoons walnut oil

This miso-kale sauce is delicious used as a dressing for salads and as a dip with raw vegetables. Here, it gives character to quinoa.

Rinse the quinoa in a fine sieve.

In a medium saucepan over a low heat, sauté the onion and mushrooms in the olive oil until the mushroom juices have almost evaporated.

Add the quinoa, bay leaves and stock to the saucepan and top up with cold water (you should have approximately 1½ times the volume of the quinoa). Bring to a simmer and cook for 10 minutes. Stir in the kale leaves, cover and leave to stand for 5 minutes.

Meanwhile, prepare the miso sauce: in a medium bowl, massage the kale and mix with the miso. Add the tofu and dress with the walnut oil.

Serve the warm quinoa topped with the miso sauce.

RISOTTO WITH KALE, NUTS AND MUSHROOMS

The kale is unadorned in this recipe and, when finely chopped, acts as an aromatic herb.

SERVES 4

1 large onion, peeled and chopped

500 g button or wild mushrooms, halved or quartered

1 tablespoon olive oil

600 ml vegetable stock

250 g arborio rice

1 tablespoon almond or cashew purée

80 g kale leaves, finely chopped

Finely grated zest and juice of 1 lemon

70 g walnuts, crushed

Grated Parmesan cheese, to serve

In a medium saucepan, sauté the onion and mushrooms in the hot oil until the mushrooms have rendered their juices. Meanwhile, heat the vegetable stock in another saucepan.

Once the mushrooms are cooked, add the rice and stir until the grains become translucent. Pour over a ladle of stock. Continue to add stock as the previous ladle is absorbed. Cooking the rice will take about 17 minutes (you may not need all the stock).

About 3 minutes before the end of cooking, add the nut purée to the risotto and stir well. Then add the kale, half the lemon juice with a few pinches of zest and the walnuts.

Serve hot, with optional Parmesan.

GOOD TO KNOW: The juice and zest of the lemon give this risotto a little pep and form an ideal accompaniment for the mushrooms.

OVEN-COOKED KALE CHIPS

SEASONINGS

Salt and vinegar: a little
vinegar and less oil

Lemon and pepper:
2 tablespoons lemon
juice and a little less oil;
salt and pepper

Garlic: 1 or 2 cloves
crushed and mixed in oil

Curry: a sprinkling of
curry powder or garam
masala

Cheese: grated
Parmesan and add
another few minutes
cooking time

Cinnamon and maple
syrup: 1 tablespoon
each coconut oil and
maple syrup, 1 teaspoon
cinnamon

Chocolate: 1 tablespoon
coconut or olive oil,
1½ tablespoons sugar,
1½ tablespoons cocoa
powder

This is a classic kale recipe, and the one that has won over the most die-hard I-don't-do greens people. Devilishly crusty, these chips are nutritionally impeccable and quick to prepare.

Preheat the oven to 170°C/Gas mark 3.

Spread out a few washed and dried kale leaves across an oven tray. Drizzle lightly with olive oil and a sprinkle of sea salt.

Massage the kale leaves with your fingers so that each one is covered with oil and salt.

Bake for 10 minutes and leave to cool before eating.

GOOD TO KNOW: Everything about these oven-cooked kale chips is good, so feel free to play around with the different seasonings. The sweet seasonings need double the cooking time, because the sugary elements tend to add more liquid to the mix.

KALE FETA CIGARS

I was inspired by Middle-Eastern cuisine to create a rich, green filling for filo pastry. Here, kale replaces the more traditional greens like chard, spinach, mint and parsley and marries just as beautifully with the feta.

SERVES 4

1 tablespoon olive oil, plus extra for brushing

100 g kale leaves, finely chopped

1 courgette, trimmed and diced

1 teaspoon sumac

200 g feta, crumbled

120 g nuts, crushed

8 sheets filo pastry

Preheat the oven to 200°C/Gas mark 6. Warm the olive oil in a medium saucepan and add the kale and courgette. Cover, lower the heat and leave for 15 minutes, then drain.

Mix the vegetables with the sumac, feta and crushed nuts. Divide the filling equally between the filo sheets, placing it along the width of each sheet.

Turn the edges of each filo sheet inwards, brush with olive oil and roll up like a cigar. Bake on a non-stick tray for 10 minutes. Serve warm.

KALE AND SOYA BALLS

This recipe makes around 20 meatballs. You can top them with a hot tomato sauce or the creamy avocado sauce on page 33. They also go well with a green salad or a plate of vegetables.

SERVES 4

45 g textured soya protein

3 tablespoons soy sauce

70 g oats or spelt

2 tablespoons chia seeds

100 g mashed vegetables (pumpkin, potato, sweet potato)

Small handful of kale leaves, finely chopped

30 g ground almonds

3 tablespoons chestnut flour

Olive oil

Salt

Preheat the oven to 180°C/Gas mark 4.

Place the soya protein in a large bowl and mix with soy sauce. Cover with boiling water and leave to stand for at least 30 minutes, then drain. Meanwhile, cover the oats and chia seeds with 150 ml of boiling water and leave to stand for 15 minutes.

In a blender, combine the drained soya, oats and chia seeds with the mashed vegetables and a pinch of salt. Blend without making too smooth. Add the finely chopped kale, ground almonds and flour. Blend again.

Make each meatball the size of a large walnut. Place on a greased baking tray and bake for 15 minutes.

GOOD TO KNOW: If you prefer, you can shape this mix into six burgers and serve them in buns with salad, pickles and ketchup.

KALE, GOAT'S CHEESE AND SWEET POTATO TART

Kale and sweet potato make a great combination, each of them mellow and sweet in their own way. The cheese adds texture and zing.

SERVES 6

100 g wholegrain rice flour

20 g potato starch

80 g cornflour

Pinch of salt

1 egg

40 ml olive oil or ghee

For the filling

1 sweet potato, peeled and diced

100 g fresh goat's cheese

1 egg

Pinch of salt

50 g kale leaves, finely chopped

Preheat the oven to 180°C/Gas mark 4.

In a large bowl, mix together the flour, potato starch, cornflour and salt. Incorporate the egg and oil or ghee. Work the mixture to a sand between your fingers. If necessary add a few drops of water.

Without kneading the pastry, use it to line a 20-cm flan dish, pressing the mix down into the dish with the palm of your hand.

To make the filling, first steam the sweet potato for 15 minutes. Mash it with the goat's cheese, egg and salt. Work the chopped kale into the mix.

Fill the tart base and bake for about 35 minutes. Serve hot, cold or warm – all are just as lovely

GOOD TO KNOW: The tart base in this recipe is gluten-free.

KALE, SWEET POTATO AND RED LENTIL SOUP

An invigorating winter soup to serve with a slice of grilled bread. The lentils and root vegetables take on the flavours of the miso and coconut. For a gourmand variation you might add a few cubes of smoked tofu.

SERVES 4

1 teaspoon coconut oil

1 onion, peeled and finely diced

4 carrots, peeled and finely diced

1 sweet potato, peeled and finely diced

75 g red lentils

3 bay leaves

1 tablespoon miso

470 g can of tomatoes and their juice

1 stick fresh turmeric, peeled and crushed

3 generous handfuls of kale leaves, chopped

100 ml coconut milk

Warm the oil in a large pan. Add the diced vegetables and sweat over a medium heat for a few minutes. Add the lentils, 400 ml water and bay leaves.

As the water comes to the boil, blend in the miso and the tomatoes. Cover and leave to cook for 20 minutes, long enough for the vegetables to become tender.

Add the turmeric, chopped kale and coconut milk. Cook gently for another 5 minutes.

GOOD TO KNOW: Lightly chopped and added at the end of the cooking time, the kale has just enough time to cook while keeping all its nutrition.

DOUBLE KALE PIZZA

Here, kale features as a pesto in the dough and on top of the pizza as if it were rocket. Note that the dough is rich in grains and contains a little white flour, a bit like a fine Neapolitan pizza dough.

SERVES 4

250 g spelt flour, plus 150 g for dusting

2 teaspoons salt

10 g dried yeast

3 tablespoons olive oil

2 tablespoons seeds – sunflower, sesame, chia, linseed, etc.

For the topping

1 tablespoon olive oil

2 shallots, peeled and diced

250 g mushrooms, sliced

1 serving kale pesto (see page 30)

2 balls of mozzarella cheese, sliced

30 g kale leaves, finely chopped

4 tablespoons lemon juice

Place the flour in a large bowl. Add the salt, yeast and olive oil. Pour in 250 ml warm water and add the seeds.

Knead by hand for 10 minutes. Cover and leave to rest in a warm spot for one hour.

For the topping, warm the oil in a pan and sweat the shallots gently. Add the mushrooms and cook until almost dry. Set aside.

Flour a work surface and knock the dough back with the palm of your hand and then shape into a ball again. Do this a few times. Roll out flat on to non-stick baking paper.

Smear on the kale pesto, then add the sweated shallots and mushrooms. Lay the mozzarella slices on top.

Leave everything to rest while the oven warms up to 180°C/ Gas mark 4. Bake for 15 minutes.

Once cooked, sprinkle the pizza with the finely chopped kale and lemon juice. Serve hot.

KALE LASAGNE WITH BUTTERNUT SQUASH

The secret of vegetarian lasagne is to get the right balance of each layer – a smooth purée of vegetables, lightly but carefully seasoned, a layer of pasta, and a creamy cheese. And the other key ingredient is very good tomato sauce.

SERVES 4

500 g butternut squash, peeled, seeds removed and sliced

200 ml creamed oats or double cream

300 ml tomato sauce

9 sheets of lasagne, fresh or pre-cooked

75 g kale leaves, chopped

100 g goat's cheese, crumbled

Grated Parmesan cheese, to finish

Salt and pepper

Steam the squash slices for 20 minutes, then mash in a large mixing bowl. Mix in 150 ml creamed oats or double cream. Season to taste.

Cover the base of a gratin dish with a thin layer of tomato sauce (about 150 ml) and cover with three sheets of lasagne. Cover these with a layer of the squash mix. Place another three sheets of lasagne over the top.

Mix the kale with the cheese and the rest of the creamed oats. Spread this over the top of the lasagne and place the remaining three lasagne sheets on top of that. Finish with a layer of tomato sauce. Sprinkle the Parmesan on top.

Preheat the oven to 180°C/Gas mark 4 and bake the lasagne for 35 minutes. Leave to stand for 10 minutes before serving.

GOOD TO KNOW: This lasagne is easily assembled the night before serving and kept in the refrigerator until needed for cooking.

STEAMED GREEN BREAD

This ultra-soft bread is incredibly simple to make, as well as quick to prove and cook. The steaming preserves both the colour and nutrients of the kale. The bread is delicious with farmhouse butter and a cheese platter.

SERVES 6

50 g kale leaves, chopped

1 tablespoon brown sugar

½ teaspoon sea salt flakes

1 tablespoon olive oil

170 g wheat flour or white spelt flour

1 tablespoon dried baker's yeast

1 tablespoon instant yeast

In a blender, combine the kale with 90 ml warm water, the sugar, salt and oil to make a coarse purée. Add 50 g flour and blend again to achieve a smooth purée.

Transfer the purée to a large bowl. Add the remaining flour and the two yeasts and knead for at least 5 minutes. Shape into a ball, cover and leave to rise in a warm place for one hour.

Once risen, shape the dough to the desired form (rolls or plaited bread, for example). Place on a sheet of non-stick baking paper placed in the bottom of a steamer.

Cover and leave to rise for 45 minutes. Steam for 30 minutes and leave to stand for 15 minutes without lifting the lid.

INDEX